I0115635

A GRAND VISION

ACADEMIC MORALITY IV

SEMISI PONE
BSc, MSc (Hons)

Copyright © Rainbow Enterprises Books, 2019

Publisher: Rainbow Enterprises Books, 2019

ISBN: 978-1-98-851145-0

All rights reserved. No part of this book shall be
reproduced, in any way, without prior written
permission from the writer and copyright holder.

Rainbow Enterprises Books is a division of
Rainbow Enterprises and Investments 7 Ltd, a
registered company in New Zealand.

CONTENTS

Chapters

1. Land Administration...4
2. Agriculture and Export Improvement...14
3. Inmigration Tourism...28
4. Harnessing creativity...31
5. The Case for Estate Commercialization...38

   Notes on the author...43

INTRODUCTION

After 30 years of Politics and blowing the trumpet of good governance, it is time to improve the administration. We cannot spent all our time trying to improve good governance while everything else fall apart.

In this ebook, I shall put forward some ideas to improve the current operations. The Tongan Government should invest some time looking at those options and others for improving the problems raised and also the economic well being of the country. Good governance works when everything works well. If the country is falling to pieces because of poor government management then what is the point of talking about good governance?

The author also puts forward his opinions and ideas about how we should envisage improvement in the economic situation.

As a former farmer and agriculture expert in Tonga, the author feels that 'a grand vision' is what Tonga needs to escape the never ending trade deficits.

In the spirit of the first 3 books of this series, it is hoped that these discussions will contribute towards the Democratic process in Tonga. In addition, a cooperative atmosphere be developed between the Democratic and Traditional supporters for the betterment of the islands and the future of its children.

Chapter 1....

Land Administration

Good governance means that we do all that is required for the proper functioning of the country. We do not just pay lip service to good governance and do nothing…or worse do the opposite.

I would like to discuss some issues that clearly demonstrate that what we need in Tonga is not good governance but good administration.

Issue Number 1.

My family have land in Tonga and we have a lot of problems administering it because of the lack of infrastructure and the right kind of service. For example, there is no commercial company handling the rents of properties or manage them. There was a small company doing it, in the past 30 years, but they only take properties that will give them a large profit. I am not sure whether they are still in business.

This is the question.

If land/property rental service is not available, then it is the government's responsibility to ensure somebody does it. Without that service there will be no progress in property development like (i) Rental Housing Investments (ii) Small Motels/Hotels/Resorts which local Tongans can do. This would encourage international big players to move in and take over the local tourism industry. This has happened in every island around the world. **Tonga should try and avoid this by encouraging its own people to invest in property development….by providing the rental and collection services for Tongan owners who may be living overseas.**

The Tongan Government is always looking for ways to raise revenue and this should be a good income stream for the country. The Tongan Government, through the Ministry of Lands and Survey is already collecting money from land leases, survey costs, land registration, deed of ownership production and so on. Why not add another service which is **collection of rents on behalf of overseas Tongan owners** who have invested money building on their land? This service will benefit the country in several ways;

1. Increase investments by overseas Tongans in Tonga.
2. Generate jobs from all the new houses being built.
3. Generate jobs from the tourism businesses/resorts/motels being built.
4. Increase visits by overseas Tongans and the money generated from their purchases and cash gifts to family and relatives.
5. Eliminate the large number of 'neglected properties' which a a huge 'eyesore' in many of the villages.

I have tried to interest my relatives in helping manage my properties in Tonga, for 20 years or so, but there is always a problem. They are neither trained nor financially able to do it.

Issue Number 2.

Abandoned Housing

There are dozens of examples of problems in this area. If you drive through the villages in Tongatapu, you can see some really nice houses that are abandoned and needs repair/occupancy. If Government makes it easy to rent and collect rent, it will generate cash for everybody and there will be no abandoned empty houses in the villages and towns. **It is a win-win-win situation.** The Government wins, the land owners win and the people employed in these enterprises win.

Here are two cases from my family.

Case Number 1.

Squatters…

My father build a small house on my property in a village on the East side of Tongatapu. The house is probably 5 metres by 15 metres. I have been giving money to my parents since working in Samoa (University of the South Pacific) and Fiji (South Pacific Commission) and I guess they had some surpluses. There were people living in the house when I first visited after we moved to New Zealand in 1996. I asked them to move out as I intend to extend it and rent it out. In the meantime, I left it with my cousin to look after. My cousin found a friend who was willing to live there and look after the property. I asked my cousin if they can pay rent of $20 a week since they are selling goods on the main roadside and making money from living on the property.There are, at least, 200 vehicles passing through there every day. Many of them stop and buy goods. The road is the only main road to the East of the Eastern District of Tongatapu. The population of the area is probably the biggest on the island so the property is perfectly located. Anyone doing business there will make good income every day. My neighbors have been running a flea market on the roadside for years and they said on a good day they make up to $400 pa'anga selling clothes, ag-produce (taro leaves, boiled corn, root crops).

Because of the problem of communication I drafted a rental agreement and send it with my niece who came to visit us in Auckland in

2015-2016. I requested the occupants to pay $50 a week rent. The size of the property is 1,500 square metres so they can do many businesses from there. After 5 years I still have not heard anything. What has happened?

I have made verbal requests and also send a written agreement…but nothing! **I see it as a government administration problem made worse by apathy of the local population.**

Firstly, there should be laws to protect property owners. Second the government should have a department that oversees rental arrangements. Thirdly, the **village chief** should ensure that the property owners on his estate should get a fair deal. I should have collected $7,000 on a rental of $20 or $18,200 on a rental of $50 a week in the last 5 years. The rules and regulations in the villages is too 'easy going' and people just please themselves.

In New Zealand a property that size (1,500sqm) in Auckland will be collecting, at least, $500 a week in rent. There is no **squatter problem** in New Zealand. If you set up camp on somebody else's land the Police will be asked to evict you within 24 hours or so.

I have talked to the young couple, who live on my property, in Nuku'alofa. They came to see me with some fruits and seafood. To be fair, I

9

did tell them they can stay there until I can give them a rental agreement. I was very sick at the time, in Nuku'alofa, and in no position to do much. I returned to Auckland as a result. That was in February, 2015.

It does show that the couple living on my property may not be bad people, but they are also in no position to do anything. Whose fault is it? I have sent the agreement, but they probably did not get it.

This is why there should be a website operated by the Tongan Government where the Village Chief (or appointed official), Tenants and Landlord can do things like agreements and payments. This can add much cash and developmental goodwill to the Tongan Government's list of business operations.

I now plan to travel to Tonga and sort out the problem myself. My sister also has a rental property in Nuku'alofa and she is complaining all the time about the actions of the locals.

Case Number 2.

Builders who don't keep their word and contract agreement.

While I was working as the Plant Protection Advisor and Co-ordinator of the Plant Protection

Service for the South Pacific Commission in Fiji (1993-1996), I decided to build a rental property in Nuku'alofa on a leased piece of land from my family.

I visited Nuku'alofa, from Suva, and signed a contract with a local builder. He asked for $1,000 to do 'the floor plan'.. At the time I could buy a 'map/floor plan' for $200. Because the builder will draw the floor plan according to my specification, I did not mind paying five times the normal price.

I made some arrangements with the Bank of Tonga and requested a loan of $80,000 to build the house. It was pre-approved, by the Bank of Tonga, awaiting the 'house map/floor plan' which is a requirement before the money is released.

The builder did not finish the map/floor plan after one year! I made some inquiries and he said he has been busy planting tomatoes! I cannot believe it. *I have wasted more than one year and nothing has happened. I was close to the end of my contract with the South Pacific Commission and was planning to migrate to New Zealand in 1995-1996.*

I asked my lawyer, Mr Sosefo Hola r.i.p. and Sefo advised I should sue him. We have a contract and he was in breach of the contract conditions. I agreed. Sefo gave the builder notice that we will seek compensation in the Tonga High Court.

A week later I received a letter from the builder apologizing…saying he was sorry…he said he was sick and he sent me the half finished map/floor plan. He was asking for forgiveness. I have no choice but to forgive him like a good school mate. We went to the same high school (Tonga High School)….and relative. My father is also related to his father…so in Tongan style I forgave him and the case was closed.

I could have made $400,000 in rent in the past 23 years if that rental house was built. It just show that in Tonga sometimes even the best plans fail because the people hired to do it are not the best people for the job. *It must be said that Tonga is still very backward in some ways. Most Tongan workers, and even Government Architects, do not have the work ethics of a palangi (European), for example.*

The builder is now a Minister of the Free Wesleyan Church. I really wonder what he is doing there. He should have build my house for free to save his reputation…. which is probably why he is not a builder anymore. He was a Government Architect!

I also see this as another Tongan Government problem. My contract with the builder should have been registered in a Government Office for the purpose. Government Officials should oversee this kind of agreement and development. In 1993-1996, a $80,000 rental building is a fairly large one by Tongan standards. Somebody should have been responsible to see it through….the project will generate many local jobs and support a lot of local business.

Chapter 2....

Agriculture and Export Improvement

Tonga is steadily increasing exports of fish ($5million, Tonga Stats, 2011) and root crops ($2million, Tonga Stats, 2011) but crop exports like vanilla has taken a dive. According to Tonga Stats, 2011 only $500,000 was earned from vanilla in that year. FAOSTAT has a figure of 144 tonnes of cured beans in 2006 *which would equate to $NZ 201,600,000 at the Auckland retail price of $1,400 per kilo. Single vanilla beans are sold for $6-$7 in the shops in Auckland.* FAOSTAT also show a figure of 186 tonnes for 2014, so why is Tonga Stats figure for vanilla income so very low in 2011?

Squash is making $2 million and Kava, $800,000 (Tonga Stats, 2011). It does mean that there is space for improvement. I am sure MAFF knows all about the problems.

I would like to comment further on the vanilla production. Back in the year 1988, the acreage of vanilla was about 2,000 acres (according to MAFF records) and export of cured vanilla beans was around 20 tonnes. That is a very low production figure.

EXPECTED PRODUCTION FROM 2,000 ACRES

My research on vanilla suggest that a healthy vanilla plant, after 3 years, would produce about 400 grams of green beans on average. Thus working out the expected production in cured beans is *400gms x 1,000 (plants per acre) x 2,000 (acres)/1,000 (gm per tonne)/1,000 kg/tonne/5green kg per cured kilo*. The answer is 160 tonnes of cured beans. **We expect that Tonga should be producing 160 cured tonnes of vanilla from 2,000 acres of healthy plantations.** What is it that is holding back production at below 20 cured tonnes for export? That is the damage the virus is doing. From all the information we can conclude that the losses due to the VNPV (vanilla necrosis potyvirus) is 87.5%. That is very, very high.

The FAOSTAT report of 144 tonnes in 2006 suggest there has been a huge improvement. But why is production falling in 2011? The FAOSTAT report for 2014 is 186 tonnes. It does mean that the figures from Tonga Statistic Website is wrong! Only $500,000 earned from vanilla in 2011?

Improvement

The first improvement that need to be done is to ensure the records are correct. If Tonga exported 144 tonnes of cured beans in 2006 (FAOSTAT) and 186 tonnes of cured beans in 2014 (FAOSTAT) but only earned $537,000 (Tonga Stats) from vanilla export in 2011 there is clearly lots of missing data!

Access to Finance

The next improvement that need to be made is to improve the access of locals to finance. I know that all Tongan Civil Servants have access to bank loans for various personal items. When I was a staff of Tonga MAFF (June,1985-March,1992), I had good credit at the Bank of Tonga. For example, I got a bank loan to buy a $6,500 second hand car which allow me to drive to work

from Nuku'alofa to the MAFF Research
Farm at Vaini.

I tried to get a loan at the Tonga
Development Bank, in 2010, for a
commercial agriculture export project but
I cannot get the $20,000 I asked for. I
need to have a Civil Servant as
co-borrower. The idea is for the Civil
Servant to start payments of the loan in 2
weeks from release of the money. It is a
good arrangement on the banks part but
unfortunate for me because I cannot find
any Civil Servant who will be a willing
partner. I have good security for the loan
which was my tax allotment valued at
$30,000 and I have shown the bank a
copy of the Deed of Ownership. The
major problem was, the bank officer told
me, that it was allowed in the past for
Tongans living in New Zealand to borrow
without a co-borrower in Tonga, but too
many of them *got the money and ran*
and never repaid it.

I believe that the $30,000 land security
should have been enough for me to get

the loan on my own steam. If I reneged on the agreement, the bank can 'lease out' my 8.25 acre tax allotment until they recover their money. After which my land will be returned to me. That is a 'watertight' security arrangement but it was probably the 'bosses' who made the rules and so the bank officer cannot do anything else other than follow the rules.

My experience in Tonga is such that most Tongan Officials prefer to follow the traditional line of authority. They do not like to stick their necks out or 'go out on a limb' on making decisions. It is good in a way, but it also limits the development of the country. As they say in global entrepreneurial circles, *'You cannot succeed without taking on the risks'*. My project would have enabled me to create a new market for Tongan root crops, in New Zealand, and also employ a lot of locals in Tonga, as well as help my family. Now the Auckland market, I was targeting, has been taken over by Indian cassava. Tonga's produce unfortunately, will never be sold in that market.

ROOT CROP DEVELOPMENT

Rootcrops is second only to Fish Exports at $2,318,000 (Tonga Stats, 2011) in terms of export income.

Root Crop Exports can easily be increased to $NZ10 million or more in New Zealand sales. I have made this statement in my book PLANT PROTECTION IN THE PACIFIC (amazon.com), which was published many years ago, and I will reiterate it here. There are those who **preach falsely** that the Auckland Market will be flooded with Tongan root crops. I have always laughed at such statements in the past simply because Tonga cannot produce enough to supply the Auckland Market and never will. There are close to 2 million people in Auckland, in 2019, and many of them buy and consume Pacific Root crops. Samoa and Fiji supply more than $NZ50 million (about 800-1,000 x 20 tonne containers), per year, of fresh taro and frozen cassava to New Zealand (and

Australia) so I don't see how Tonga can flood the New Zealand market with the 50-60 x 20 tonne containers it exports per year *(worth about $2 million)*. Even if Tonga exports 100 containers per year it will still fall short of demand. Where's my proof? I did point out in my book PLANT PROTECTION IN THE PACIFIC that India is now supplying cassava to the New Zealand market. Vietnam is supplying taro and yam in the New Zealand market. Why? Because Tonga, Samoa and Fiji cannot supply the market! Many of my Tongan friends and relatives are buying the Indian cassava. They say it is better than the Tongan and Fijian cassava. They also buy the Vietnamese taro and yam for their feasts on birthdays and weddings because they are the only root crops available in their area in Auckland.

….And it is beginning to look like banana export with Tonga, Samoa and Fiji losing out to bigger suppliers like India and Vietnam, *like they lost the banana export to Ecuador and the Phillipines in the previous 4 decades.*

I started importing Fijian cassava in 1996. I think I was the only supplier of Fijian cassava in Auckland. I also planted cassava in Tonga for supply in New Zealand. The problem was a Samoan ordered 2 containers of coconuts (60,000 nuts) from me which he cannot pay. It destroyed my business because I spent $22,000 and was never repaid. The Samoan went out of business. Even though he had 2 properties he was up to his neck in debt….but still he could have paid me later….after 22 years he still has not paid.

I was in a position to dominate the Root Crop Market but sadly exited too soon. This is the problem with Pacific Islanders, we tend to sabotage each others business which allows the major players to take over the market. This is exactly what is happening now. India and the bigger suppliers, like Vietnam, can easily push Tonga, Samoa and Fiji aside and dominate the market. Look whose supplying the bananas now! The Pacific Islands used to supply 100% of the New Zealand Ripe Banana Market. Now they supply 0%. The Pacific Island suppliers lost their banana supplier status to Ecuador and the Phillipines because they cannot compete. **The Pacific Islands are too small, too weak financially, and not skilled enough to take on the bigger suppliers like Ecuador and the Phillipines.**

> **The Ripe Banana Market is worth $NZ 150-200 million in New Zealand according to 2016 figures in the News Media.**

We may also lose our root crops supplier status to India and Vietnam. That is a $50-$100 million market (my estimate) in New Zealand and Australia. I said it many years ago and will say it again, in case our growers are getting forgetful.

QUALITY PROBLEMS OF TONGA EXPORTS

I visited Tonga twice between 2011 and 2015. I had a discussion with two Deputy Directors of Agriculture, Dr Viliami Manu and Mrs Losaline Ma'asi. The purpose was to ascertain the MAFF's programme regarding root crops and also to inform them of the problems of Tongan root crops in Auckland so they can do something about it.

I did discover than Tonga has a world class facility at Queen Salote Wharf which is available for grower's on Tongatapu to use. Dr Viliami Manu did make the comment that it was *underused* because growers prefer doing it in their own backyards.

I was pleased, however, that after our discussion one of the major problems was addressed. Tongans tend to use onion sacks which exposed the root crops, like peeled frozen cassava and yams, to dust and small debris. It has been a problem for many years. After our discussions, I noticed that only food grade plastic was used in the latter exported cassava, yam and taro from Tonga to Auckland.

There is more to be done as I shall explain in the last Chapter of why we should commercialize all the estates held by the Lords.

VANILLA DEVELOPMENT

I have read the sad news of the two companies propping up Tongan Vanilla arguing and threatening court cases against each other. I say it is sad news because we tend to forget that Tonga produces less than 5% of the global supply of natural vanilla beans. We should not be fighting each other, we should be helping each other to improve our share of the global market.

Tonga has done everything right in terms of developing the Vanilla Industry, up to now. It needs to do more. In my studies of the three viruses of vanilla in Tonga as

a Plant Pathologist and Senior Plant
Virologist for MAFF (1986-1992) I have
made recommendations to MAFF about
the control of the severe virus called
Vanilla Necrosis Potyvirus (VNPV) but
we do need to eliminate the other two
viruses as well. They are Odontoglossum
Ringspot Virus (ORSV) and Cymbidium
Mosaic Virus (CyMV). They do not
appear to harm the vanilla plants but we
know they cause stunted or reduced
growth in other plants. The University of
the South Pacific, Institute for Research,
Extension and Training in Agriculture
(IRETA) Tissue Culture Lab had some
healthy vanilla plants which were
duplicated at the South Pacific
Commission (now known as the
Secretariat for the Pacific Community)
Tissue Culture Lab. I was in charge of
vanilla at IRETA and also the SPC Lab
(April, 1992-May, 1996). Tonga should
request some healthy vanilla plants from
SPC and IRETA and grow them in a
quarantined area, or nursery, for supply to
the Tongan Vanilla Growers, and slowly
replace all the Vanilla plants in the

Kingdom with the new virus free cuttings. This is a very important prerequisite to any massive increase in acreage plantings for the future. The two companies buying and exporting Tongan vanilla should seriously think about doing it themselves as it would ensure a 'virus free' vanilla industry. Production would be much higher and losses due to vanilla dieback, for example, is reduced.

The other improvement that Tonga MAFF need to implement immediately is the replanting of diseased vanilla plants. ALL VNPV symptomatic plants must be replaced with healthy cuttings across the country. This would be a repeat of what we did in 1989-1991. We removed all VNPV symptomatic vanilla plants from all plantations in the Kingdom and replaced them with healthy cuttings.

This has allowed the Tonga Vanilla Industry to progress and produce much more than pre-1991 levels of production. Prior to 1991, vanilla cured bean production was less than 30 tonnes of cured beans although 160 tonnes was expected from the acreage. Now we can see that vanilla cured bean has jumped to 144 tonnes in 2006 (FAOSTAT) and 186 tonnes (FAOSTAT) simply because we removed the biggest limiting factor....Vanilla Necrosis Potyvirus.

Chapter 3....

Inmigration Tourism

Inmigration is a term I have coined to describe the Tongan Overseas tourists. In 2015, Tongan Statistics put the returning locals, by air, at 31,517 (Tongatapu). That is 30% of the total number of visitors in 2015. The total number of visitors (tourists) to Tongatapu, who arrived by air, were 53,752. The total including all islands was 104,070. We can see that the number of returning residents and visitors have surpassed the local population of 101,000 back in 2015. It does mean there is a large amount of cash the visitors bring in.

The point of this explanation is that there are about 300,000 Tongans living overseas who can come as visitors to Tonga or inmigrators. They usually bring large amounts of cash as presents for family and friends and it will contribute to the local economy. How do we get more Tongans to visit? Well, **give**

**overseas Tongans a good reason to
visit.**

**Here are some good reasons for
overseas Tongans to come to Tonga;**

1. **Investment** - Create an environment
where overseas Tongans can come and
invest in Tonga. Perhaps by offering
brochures of available investments in the
country. One example would be;
(i) If a resort and local/Tongan property
developer in Tonga need money for his
project, he can offer a brochure with
investment opportunities for Tongans to
buy shares in the resort. The Government
should set up a department to handle and
record such transactions and also
guarantee such investments. That is very
important. If the Tongan Government
does not handle the investments and
guarantee them the scheme might fall
over. It need that kind of security for
investors to have confidence in it.

2. **Targeting** - It would be very easy for
the Tongan Government to get the

addresses of every Tongan living overseas and send them a 'special' every year to come and visit Tonga. For example, free accommodation, free food, special trips, special local cruises to the outer islands and so on. They can send them by email which would cost very little. The Tourism Department should handle such promotions. I know this will work judging from events in my childhood. Every time my uncles, aunties or cousins visit from overseas there is usually a large amount of cash spent buying vehicles, building houses and even distributing cash and new clothes. I have now lived overseas for 27 years and I know the Tongans and people of Tongan descent, in New Zealand for example, would love to co-own a resort of be offered a holiday from Tongan hotels and motels.

Chapter 4....

Harnessing Creativity

In terms of harnessing creativity, King Taufa'ahau Tupou IV had the best idea. He established Tonga High School with the view of harnessing the creativity and brain power of his people. When I was a young boy, it was my father's dream that I would attend Tonga High School. I did successfully pass my exams and entered Tonga High School in 1974. I did realize that every parent had tried very hard to get their children there.

Many of my fellow students in Tonga High School were from the islands and they migrated with their parents to Nuku'alofa or one of the villages in Tongatapu so they can attend Tonga High School.

I often wonder what it is that make Tonga High School different. They have the best teachers, the best school building but that was about it. I did learn a little about music and art. I learned a bit more about carpentry and woodworking as extra skills but no earth shattering changes that I could boast of.

I was the only Tongan boy that passed New Zealand School Certificate in 5 subjects (1978) and University Entrance in 5 subjects (1979). Perhaps that is something I can boast about. There were hundreds of kids, from around the country, sitting the exams and I was the only one who passes all of them…and I was from Tonga High School. That must be it. I have better skills and academic ability because I went to Tonga High School. But there were about 100 Tonga High School students who sat the exam too. Some of those students who did not pass in 5 subjects passed in 4 , 3 or 2 subjects, now have Bachelor, Masters and PhDs degrees and have good jobs. The fact they did not pass their English in NZ School Certificate or University Entrance did not stop them from succeeding later in life. English seem to be the stumping block for them….but English was one of my best marks at University Entrance!

It does point out that success will come if they try. Failure at School Certificate and University Exams does not mean they stop learning or trying to get better results at degree level later.

What the King has done effectively is create a core of people whose intelligence quotient is above average. I did analyze the Tongan Civil Servant, for example, to see how many Tonga High School Students are there and it shows. Most of the top jobs, in the Tonga Civil Service, are held by Tonga High School old boys and girls. It is interesting to see it replicated in politics. The Members of Parliament people's seats are increasingly being taken by Tonga High School old boys and girls. Even the Lord's Members of Parliament are being taken over by Tonga High School old boys.

The King was right. In separating the cream of the country's children into a top school and giving them the best teachers, he was able to produce some super smart civil servants who set the standards for the kids to aspire to. I have read, at least one report (of a study/survey) where it is claimed that Tonga has the highest number of university degree holders per capita than any other country in the world. I have not analyzed this data but I can predict that 80% of them or thereabouts are Tonga High School Students.

King Taufa'ahau Tupou IV did know how to harness the country's children's creativity when he established Tonga High School in 1947.

So what do we do now? That is the question. We should build on what the King has done and develop the country's children even more. It reminds me of what Tony Blair, former Prime Minister of the United Kingdom said;

'We should develop our children to the highest extent of their potential' (in order for the country to benefit economically)

In his speech, he meant that a country that develops its children in such a way would be very, very successful in the future.

Some examples of successful students from Tonga High School;

From my generation (1974);

1. Semisi Pule also known as Semisi Pule Pone (me).

Passed NZ School Certificate (1978) and NZ University Entrance (1979) in 5 subjects at Tonga High School. Entered Mt Albert Grammar School, Auckland and passed with 240 marks (pass mark for entering Auckland University was 200) to the University of Auckland. Graduated with Bachelor of Science (May,1985) and Master of Science (Hons) (May, 1989). Worked as a Plant Pathologist and Senior Plant Virologist for MAFF, Tonga (June 1985-March 1992), Tissue Culture Fellow for IRETA, University of the South Pacific, Samoa (April 1992-May

1993). Plant Protection Advisor and Co-ordinator for the South Pacific Commision Plant Protection Service, Fiji (June 1993-May, 1996). Chief Executive for the Pacific Plant Protection Organization /SPC Secretariat. Appointed Member of the Committee of Experts for Phytosanitary Measures, FAO, United Nations (1993-2000), Italy. Now a writer with more than 200 books and ebooks in amazon.com and blurb.com. Now live in Auckland, New Zealand.

2. Dr Talaivosa Ate Foliaki Moala, Tonga High School Dux 1979, Passed NZ School Certificate (1978) and NZ University Entrance (1979) in 5 subjects at Tonga High School. Attended University of Otago where she graduated from with a MBBS. She is now a medical Doctor in Wellington, New Zealand.

3. Dr 'Ofa Afuha'amango. Passed NZ School Certificate (1978) and NZ University Entrance (1979) in 5 subjects at Tonga High School. Attended University and graduated with BA and

MA and PhD. She is now Director of Statistics at SPC (Secretariat for the Pacific Community….formerly known as South Pacific Commission) based in Noumea, New Caledonia.

4. Roger Bernabe - Passed NZ School Certificate (1978) and NZ University Entrance (1979) in 5 subjects at Tonga High School. Graduated from Auckland University with Bachelor of Science and Graduate Diploma of Science. Now works and live in Australia.

5. Lisita Kaufusi - Passed NZ School Certificate (1978) and NZ University Entrance (1979) in 5 subjects at Tonga High School.

From other generations;

1. Professor Futa Helu
2. Clive Edwards
3. Dr 'Ana Taufe'ulungaki
4. Dr Sitaleki Finau
5. Dr Viliami Manu
6. Semisi Fakahau

Chapter 5....

The Case for Estate Commercialization

This is an idea that I hope will generate some discussions.

There are **41 'Lords of the Realm'** in the Kingdom of Tonga. Before King George Tupou V installed the last 8 in 2008, there were only 33 since 1890. The qualification of those last 8 Lords were just *'outstanding performance in Tonga's Civil Service or equivalent'*. Since 1890, the qualification for being installed as a Lord was being the **heir** which can be proved by genealogy if there were no children by the previous Lord/Noble. The King can also install somebody else if he deem the **heir** is not fit or does not have enough links to the previous Lord/Noble. Each Lord, except the last eight Lords, is given a hereditary estate which he will look after including the people that live there in the villages on his estate.

Some of those estates have a large number of commercial leases that make the Lord rich from the money and assets collected. It also demonstrates that every estate can generate a lot of money for the Lord and his people but also for the country. Some villages have groups that operate in this way with the Lord as the Team Leader/Chairman.

Suppose that we have a Tonga National Plan to implement of a targeted fund raising/commercial operation for each estate of a billion dollars?. That will give the country a GDP of around 33-40 billion dollars. Would everyone support it? I am sure they will. Who will not support it? A 30-40 times increase in income for the country.

How do we go about creating a 40 billion industry based on the 34 estates that make up the Kingdom of Tonga? The 33 Lord's estate and the Government estate (the 34th).

This is an example;

1. First we register 34 companies
Chaired by each Lord or a qualified
person from his estate. These companies
will take on local business in Tonga and
overseas business in New Zealand,
Australia and USA where the majority of
overseas Tongans live. The companies
can also bid for work outside these
countries.
2. Each company will be given a
specialist task in any field it wishes. For
example, the first company will deal with
vanilla production, export, processing,
development and so on..in Tonga and
overseas. A Board of Directors is chosen
who will select experts to put together a
business plan for the company and also
write its constitution.
3. The company can use its income to
purchase assets like property, other
businesses and investments that will
create its billion dollar portfolio.
4. Another example is communication.
One company can develop local
communication in Tonga and also buy

into communication business overseas with its own products and services. Another company can take on fisheries and develop the local fishing industry, export as well as overseas investments like;

1. Building a cannery or similar business.
2. Here's a list of potential ideas for company businesses;

(i) Root crops production, processing *(for example - if you sell a 20 kg bag of frozen cassava in NZ it will fetch $40-$45 but if you convert the same bag of cassava into chips it will earn more than $200!)*

(ii) Biosecurity technology like fruit and vegetable treatment for export

(iii) Shipping

(iv) IT

(v) Construction

(vi) Ship building

(vii) Underwater construction

(viii) Tourism

(ix) Kava production and export

(x) Coconut products

(xi) Education

...and so on.

It may sound far fetched but we can study some existing models of countries who are successful.

For example, a very, very small but very, very successful country - Monaco.

The principality of Monaco.
Area - 2.2 square kilometre
Population - 38,897
GDP - $6,500,000,000 or $6.5 billion (2016)

The model of Monaco is a very successful one. A very small land area with a small population but with a very high income.

There are many others in Europe, as well.

I shall also write a follow up book on this same topic with a lot more detail.

About the author...

Semisi Pule also known as Semisi Pule Pone, uses Semisi Pone for short, was born in the island Kingdom of Tonga in the South Pacific in 1961. He attended Longolongo Primary School and Tonga High School in Tonga (1967-1979) then Mt Albert Grammar School and the University of Auckland (1980-1984) in New Zealand. He graduated with a Bachelor of Science in May 1985 and joined the Ministry of Agriculture, Fisheries and Forests in Tonga in June 1985 as an Agriculture Officer/Plant Pathologist.

He was awarded a scholarship by the German Government through GTZ, and the Tonga-German Plant Protection Project, to do a Master of Science programme doing research on the Vanilla viruses (1987-1988) at Auckland University. He graduated in may 1989, with Honours, and continued his work with MAFF.

He was appointed to the position of Senior Plant Virologist for his work on Vanilla, Kava and Squash viruses in 1991.

His work in Tonga is published in many scientific papers and his series of books and ebooks on PLANT PROTECTION IN THE PACIFIC.

In March 1992, he joined the PRAP Project 7 at IRETA, USP as a Fellow in Tissue Culture. His work there is published in the book PLANT PROTECTION IN THE PACIFIC 3, Tissue Culture.

He joined the South Pacific Commission Plant Protection Service in April 1993 as its Plant Protection Advisor and Co-ordinator of the Plant Protection Service (1993-1996). His work at the SPC PPS are published in his series of books and ebooks on PLANT PROTECTION IN THE PACIFIC.

He is now a writer with more than 200 books and ebooks in amazon.com and blurb.com.

He also operate a small contracts business.

Further Reading...

1. Academic Morality (amazon.com)
2. Academic Morality II (amazon.com)
3. Academic Morality III (amazon.com)

www.ingramcontent.com/pod-product-compliance
Lightning Source LLC
Chambersburg PA
CBHW021338290326
41933CB00038B/974

* 9 7 8 1 9 8 8 5 1 1 4 5 0 *